The Burns Braille Transcription Dictionary

The Burns Braille Transcription Dictionary

Mary F. Burns

Introduction by Toni Heinze

New York

Second printing, 1995

Printed in Canada

Library of Congress Cataloging-in-Publication Data

Burns, Mary F., date.
The Burns braille transcription dictionary / developed by Mary F. Burns.
p. cm.
ISBN 0-89128-232-7 (acid-free paper)
1. Blind--Printing and writing systems--Handbooks, manuals, etc.
I. Title. II. Title: Braille transcription dictionary.
HV1672.B87 1991 91-40378
686.2'82--dc20 CIP

This book is dedicated in loving memory to

Jean Burns
27 years was too short a time
to learn all you had to teach

and to

Robert Burns
for all your support, encouragement, and enthusiasm.
I couldn't have asked for better.

Table of Contents

Foreword

Like many other people, I became a professional in this field—specifically, a public school teacher of the visually handicapped—in a rather roundabout way. I was getting a master's degree in music education at San Francisco State University and needed a thesis topic. For inspiration, I turned to *Grove's Dictionary of Music and Musicians* and started with the *a*'s. I will never know whether *c* through *z* included topics that would have interested me, because I stopped toward the end of the *b*'s when I came to braille music. San Francisco State also had a master's program in education of the visually handicapped, so I was able to enroll in the course on braille I needed to write my music thesis. But then I fell in love. With braille. Soon, I was as fascinated by the whole process of learning without vision as I was by braille itself, and I never looked back.

Because braille brought me into the field of blindness and visual impairment, being heavily involved in the ongoing campaign to strengthen and expand braille literacy in this country has been especially rewarding for me. We at the American Foundation for the Blind (AFB) believe that teachers of blind children and adults are the keys to literacy. Thus, providing these teachers with the handy, practical tools they need to teach braille effectively is one of AFB's major priorities for the 1990s. *The Burns Braille Transcription Dictionary* is the first of what we hope are many publications and other resources AFB publishes to make the teaching of braille more effective, efficient, and fun for teachers, students, and students' families and friends. At this point, AFB would like to thank Kristin Schumann, certified braille transcriber, and Dr. Toni Heinze, associate professor, Special

Education Faculty, Northern Illinois University, for their help in reviewing the manuscript for accuracy.

Finally, I would like to point out that the *Dictionary*'s compiler, Mary Burns, is a public school teacher of the visually impaired with Cooperative Educational Service Agency #6 in Oshkosh, Wisconsin. If the braille literacy campaign we are waging is to succeed, the everyday teachers and users of braille must be its backbone, as contributors as well as supporters. We will continue to look to them for solutions.

Susan J. Spungin
Associate Executive Director
Program Services
American Foundation for the Blind

Introduction

Renewed interest in the promotion of literacy among all people in this country has brought with it renewed attention to the importance of braille literacy for children and adults who are blind. Critical components in the promotion of literacy are the skill and attitude of the teacher. The braille teacher's role is a broad one—teaching the braille code, its rules, and the application of those rules; producing accurate and appropriate materials; adapting classroom materials; and communicating a respect for braille as a medium for reading and writing. Every facet of this role involves a commitment to accuracy.

To carry out these responsibilities, teachers avail themselves of the braille skills that they learned in their personnel preparation programs, a variety of texts for reference, and current programs and strategies for teaching braille reading and writing. However, there are still times when the teacher wants a quick reference for checking hard-to-remember contractions or composition signs or for confirming their proper usage. This may be especially true for teachers who have not consistently had students or clients who would benefit from braille. Depending on which aspect of the braille code one wants to check, the process can be quick or cumbersome. *The Burns Braille Transcription Dictionary* will go a long way in helping these individuals by making these reference and accuracy checks both quick and easy.

This handy little book can be used in several ways because it has multiple access points. One can use the alphabetical index of print-to-braille contractions to find the formation of the characters involved in a particular contraction or short form ("What is the braille contraction for *young?*" or "Isn't there a braille contraction for *young?*"). This same approach can be used in a similar section on punctuation and composition signs ("What is the braille sign for a semicolon or for double quotation marks?"). One can also use the sequential order of braille-to-print cell and dot arrangements to identify a particular sign in question ("What does a 3-cell sign consisting of dots 5, 1-3-5, 1-2-4 mean?"). Finally, one can use the alphabetical listing of the print form of contractions, punctuation, and composition signs to find a concise statement of appropriate usage for those signs in braille.

Although this tool was developed by a teacher to meet a need experienced by teachers of students with visual impairments, teachers are not the only individuals who will find this dictionary useful. Teacher's aides with training in Grade 2 braille will also benefit from using the book as they assist in the production of braille materials for their students or work with these students in the regular classroom or resource room. Transcribers are another group of individuals for whom braille accuracy is of paramount importance, and as adept as they may be at referencing the Library of Congress's *Instruction Manual for Braille Transcribing,* they will find this dictionary a quick and easy-to-use tool. Parents and other family members with training in Grade 2 braille who are interested in supporting the reading and writing skills of a child or relative who is learning or using braille can use the dictionary to check their own accuracy when transcribing notes or stories or to assist the child or relative in the development of braille skills. *The Burns Braille Transcription Dictionary* is a helpful resource that offers a quick and efficient way to confirm and increase one's accuracy.

Finally, I would like to say on a more personal note that it is especially delightful to see an experienced teacher who is my former student develop and share a practical solution to a problem experienced by many teachers in their efforts to teach accurate and efficient braille skills to students and clients.

Toni Heinze
Associate Professor
Special Education Faculty
Northern Illinois University

ACKNOWLEDGMENTS

I wish to express my sincere appreciation to David R. Burns, computer consultant, Automated Concepts, Inc., Chicago, Illinois, the "supergenius" who developed the numerical system used in the "Braille to Print" section of this book and who provided me with advice and support; Joan Huntoon, educational audiologist, Green Bay Public Schools, Green Bay, Wisconsin, who makes a wonderful guinea pig; Donna St. John, graduate assistant, Department of Educational Psychology, Counseling, and Special Education, Northern Illinois University (NIU), Dekalb, Illinois, a braillist extraordinaire and a perfectionist in proofreading; Vicki Warren, vision teacher, Cooperative Educational Service Agency #6 (CESA #6), Oshkosh, Wisconsin, for her patience and support; and the staff of the Department of the Hearing Impaired, NIU, and the Six Pack from NIU.

—M.F.B.

The Burns Braille Transcription Dictionary

A Preliminary Word

As it happens with most itinerant vision teachers, for a few years I did not have anyone who read braille among my students. Then a sixth-grade student who read braille arrived in our school district. This threw me into a panic, and I spent some time brushing up on my braille skills. During this time I found myself repeatedly having to look up various symbols and rules in the *Instruction Manual for Braille Transcribing* published by the Library of Congress. We all know the eternal questions that occurred to me: "Can I use an apostrophe next to this?" "Isn't that a dot-5 contraction?" I found this process time-consuming, and yes, even tedious. I kept thinking, "There's got to be an easier way."

I started carrying the manual with me to school to prove my expertise to my student, who argued with me about rules and contractions, which I admit I encouraged. I have always had the utmost affection for the manual. Indeed, during my undergraduate years, my nights were filled with braille dreams! However, once again I was telling myself, "There's got to be an easier way."

What I wanted was something portable that I could carry easily with me. It would include a quick-look portion that would only have the braille and print equivalents with no rules, similar to braille cheat-sheet charts. It would also have a section with just a brief description of the rules and no extra information.

I thought it would be great to have a reference guide set up like those French-to-English, English-to-French pocket language dictionaries, only it would be braille-to-print, print-to-braille. I sat down at my computer and started working. A year and a half later, I had something that looked like what I had been wishing for.

It is important to remember that this book is not to be used as an instruction manual; the Library of Congress manual is used for this purpose. *The Burns Braille Transcription Dictionary* is a quick reference guide for those who already know Grade 2 braille—vision teachers, rehabilitation teachers, braille transcribers, aides, and parents. Those who know Grade 1 braille will also find it helpful for looking up Grade 1 symbols.

All of the contractions, symbols, and rules in this book were taken from *The Instruction Manual for Braille Transcribing* by Maxine B. Dorf and Earl R. Scharry, published by the Library of Congress National Library Service for the Blind and Physically Handicapped. *The Burns Braille Transcription Dictionary* can be used in conjunction with this manual and with any other manual based on the English Braille Code.

At a Glance

This section displays all the braille symbols and contractions alphabetically without any of the rules that pertain to them. The letters within parentheses have their own contractions. When a symbol is used to denote more than one meaning, all the meanings are presented. The meaning of the symbol will depend on the context in which it is used.

SYMBOLS AND CONTRACTIONS

a	⠁
about	ab
above	abv
according	ac
across	acr
after	af
afternoon	afn
afterward	afw
again	ag
against	ag(st)
ally	⠠⠽
almost	alm
already	alr
also	al
although	al(th)
altogether	alt
always	alw
ance	⠨⠑
and	⠯
ar	⠜
as	z
ation	⠠⠝
b	⠃
bb **be**	⠆
because	(be)c
before	(be)f
behind	(be)h
below	(be)l
beneath	(be)n
beside	(be)s
between	(be)t
beyond	(be)y
ble	⠼
blind	bl
braille	brl
but	b
by	⠴

c	⠉
can	c
cannot	⠸⠉
cc	⠒
ch	⠡
character	⠐⠡
child	(ch)
children	(ch)n
com	⠤
con	⠒
conceive	(con)cv
conceiving	(con)cvg
could	cd
d	⠙
day	⠐⠙
dd	⠲
deceive	dcv
deceiving	dcvg
declare	dcl
declaring	dclg
dis	⠲
do	d
e	⠑
ea	⠂
ed	⠫
either	ei
en	⠢
ence	⠰⠑

enough	⠢
er	⠻
ever	⠐⠑
every	e
f	⠋
father	⠐⠋
ff	⠖
first	f(st)
for	⠿
friend	fr
from	f
ful	⠰⠇
g	⠛
gg	⠶
gh	⠣
go	g
good	gd
great	grt
h	⠓
had	⠸⠓
have	h
here	⠐⠓
herself	h(er)f
him	hm
himself	hmf
his	⠦
i	⠊
immediate	imm

in	⠔
ing	⠬
into	⠔⠖
it	x
its	xs
itself	xf
ity	⠰⠽
j	⠚
just	j
k	⠅
know	⠐⠅
knowledge	k
l	⠇
less	⠨⠎
letter	lr
like	l
little	ll
lord	⠐⠇
m	⠍
many	⠸⠍
ment	⠰⠞
more	m
mother	⠐⠍
much	m(ch)
must	m(st)
myself	myf
n	⠝

name	
necessary	nec
neither	nei
ness	
not	n
o	
o'clock	o'c
of	
one	
oneself	(one)f
ong	
ou	
ought	
ound	
ount	
ourselves	(ou)rvs
out	(ou)
ow	
p	
paid	pd
part	
people	p
perceive	p(er)cv
perceiving	p(er)cvg
perhaps	p(er)h
q	
question	
quick	qk

quite	q
r	⠗
rather	r
receive	rcv
receiving	rcvg
rejoice	rjc
rejoicing	rjcg
right	⠐⠗
s	⠎
said	sd
sh	⠩
shall	(sh)
should	(sh)d
sion	⠨⠝
so	s
some	⠐⠎
spirit	⠸⠎
st	⠌
still	(st)
such	s(ch)
t	⠞
th	⠹
that	t
the	⠮
their	⠸⠮
themselves	(the)mvs
there	⠐⠮
these	⠘⠮
this	(th)
those	⠘⠹

through	⠐⠹
thyself	(th)yf
time	⠐⠞
tion	⠰⠝
to	⠖
today or to-day	td
together	tgr
tomorrow	tm
tonight or to-night	tn
u	⠥
under	⠐⠥
upon	⠘⠥
us	u
v	⠧
very	v
w	⠺
was	⠴
were	⠶
wh	⠱
where	⠐⠱
which	(wh)
whose	⠘⠱
will	w
with	⠾
word	⠘⠺
work	⠐⠺

world

would wd

x

y

you y

young

your yr

yourself yrf

yourselves yrvs

z

NUMBERS

1: dots 3-4-5-6, 1

2: dots 3-4-5-6, 1-2

3: dots 3-4-5-6, 1-4

4: dots 3-4-5-6, 1-4-5

5: dots 3-4-5-6, 1-5

6: dots 3-4-5-6, 1-2-4

7: dots 3-4-5-6, 1-2-4-5

8: dots 3-4-5-6, 1-2-5

9: dots 3-4-5-6, 2-4

0: dots 3-4-5-6, 2-4-5

Punctuation and Braille Symbols and Signs

This section alphabetically displays punctuation, braille symbols, and composition signs found in English braille. It also includes a general description of the rules that pertain to them. It should be remembered that, in braille, at no time will more than one space follow a punctuation symbol. Braille signs and symbols and braille composition signs refer to those symbols that are unique to braille and are not found in print.

GENERAL RULES

accent sign Used in English texts to precede letters that are printed with an accent or other mark, whether such words occur in English or anglicized words, in proper names, or in strictly foreign words, phrases, and passages. May not be used within or before a contraction, except when the accent indicates a stressed English syllable.

capital sign, single Used when only a single letter is capitalized. It always immediately precedes the letter and has priority over other composition signs.

capital sign, double Used when all the letters directly following the sign are capitalized.

italic, bold, and underline signs, single Used to indicate print italics, boldface, small capital letters, or underlining only when these are used for purposes of emphasis or distinction. Not to be used when a distinction is indicated sufficiently by other means. Must be placed immediately before the word, compound word, abbreviation, or number (and capital or number sign when used) to which the sign applies. Is not affected by an intervening hyphen, apostrophe, or the first period in an abbreviation, or when carried over to the next line. A braille manual should be consulted for specific situational rules and regulations.

italic, bold, and underline signs, double Used when more than three consecutive words are italicized, in boldface, or underlined. The first word should be preceded by the double sign and the last word must be preceded by the single sign to indicate that it is the final word in italics, in boldface, or underlined.

letter sign Used when a single letter retains its letter meaning and does not represent a contraction for a word. Must precede the letter and the capital sign when the capital sign is used. Not used for the letters "a," "i," and "o." A braille manual should be consulted for specific situational rules and regulations.

number sign Must appear before every cardinal number preceded by a space. Is not affected by intervening commas, colons, or hyphens but is affected by other punctuation, such as the dash, question mark, or parenthesis, or when carried over to the next line.

omission sign Used when dots are used in print as ellipses to indicate omitted letters.

repetition sign Used when a braille page number has been repeated. Should be inserted without a space before the repeated number.

termination sign Used to indicate that the word following a hyphen is no longer affected by the composition sign. Used only when necessary for purposes of clarity.

SYMBOLS AND SIGNS

Sign	Symbol
accent sign	
ampersand	&
apostrophe	’
asterisk	*
bracket-brace, opening	{ [
bracket-brace, closing	}]
capital-letter sign, single	
capital-letter sign, double	
cent	¢
colon	:
comma	,
dash	—

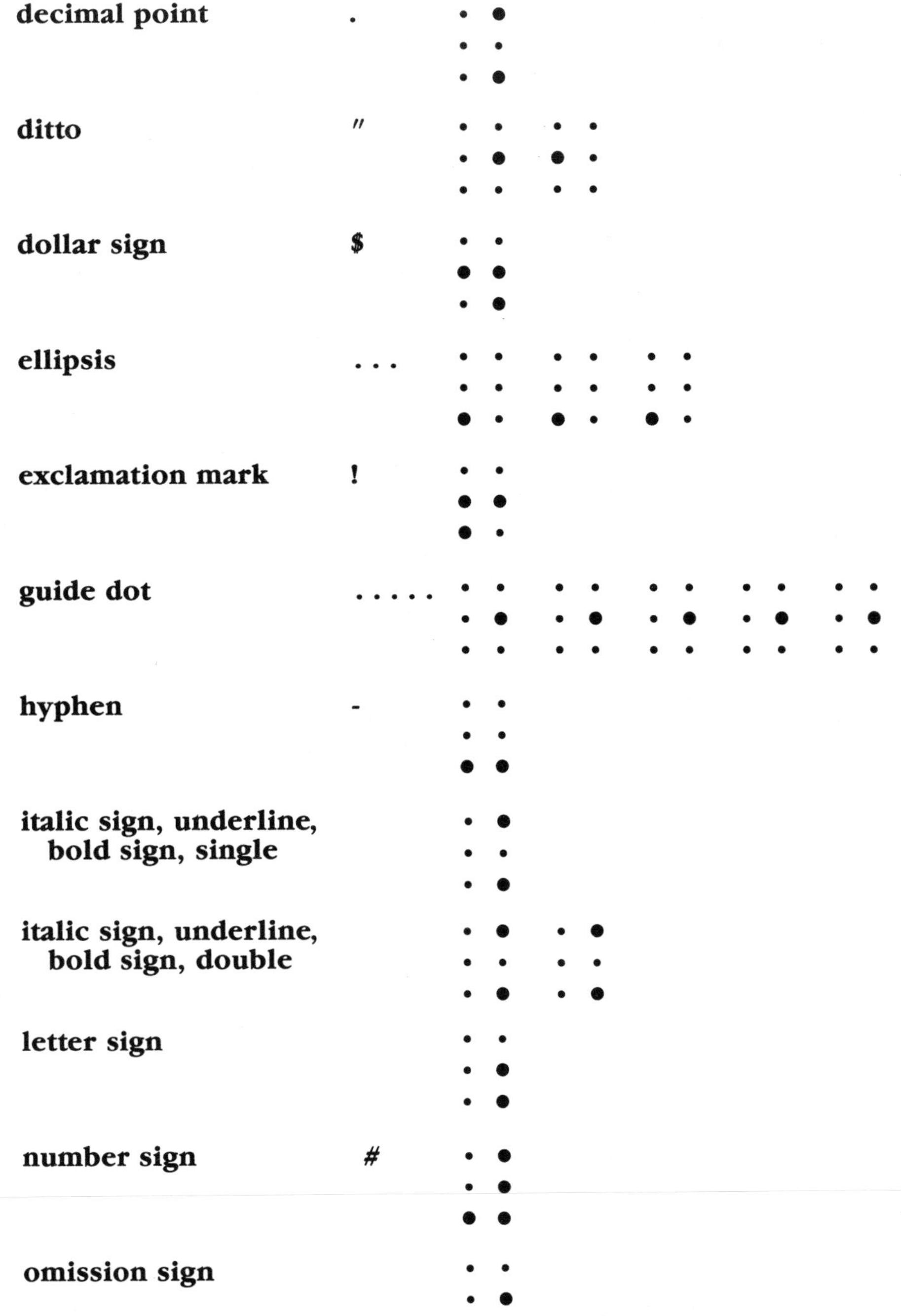

decimal point	.
ditto	〃
dollar sign	$
ellipsis	. . .
exclamation mark	!
guide dot	. . . . .
hyphen	-
italic sign, underline, bold sign, single	
italic sign, underline, bold sign, double	
letter sign	
number sign	#
omission sign	

Term	Print	Braille
parentheses, opening and closing	( )	⠶
percent	%	⠒⠏
period	.	⠲
question mark	?	⠦
quotation mark, double, opening	“	⠦
quotation mark, double, closing	”	⠴
quotation mark, single, opening	‘	⠠⠦
quotation mark, single, closing	’	⠴⠄
repetition sign		⠰
semicolon	;	⠆
slash, bar, oblique stroke, fraction line	/-	⠌
termination sign and transcriber’s note, begin and end		⠠⠄

Braille to Print

This section displays all the braille symbols and contractions alphabetically. It also includes a brief description of where they may appear in text.

The section is organized in numerical fashion on the basis of the six-dot cell system. The dots are designated as follows:

1 • • 4
2 • • 5
3 • • 6

The symbols in this section are grouped according to the number of cells the symbol uses and the number of dots used in the first cell. Within these subcategories (number of cells, number of dots), the symbols are organized numerically beginning with the first cell. For example, in the subcategory 1 cell, 2 dots, the symbols are in the following order:

Dots:

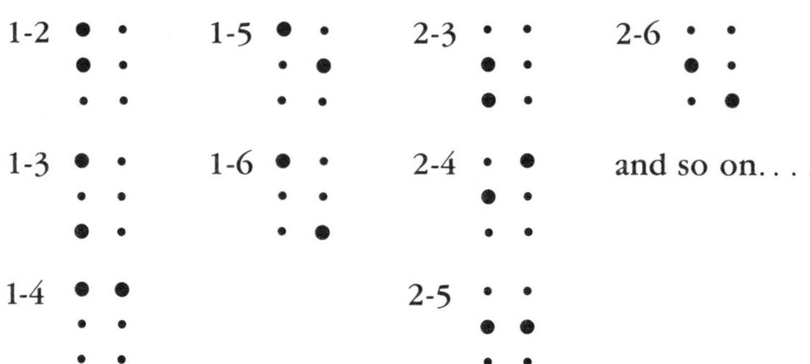

1 CELL, 1 DOT

● • • • • •	**dot 1** **a** **1** (when preceded by the number sign).
• • ● • • •	**dot 2** **ea** Part-word contraction only. , Comma.
• • • • ● •	**dot 3** ' Apostrophe.
• ● • • • •	**dot 4** ` Accent.
• • • ● • •	**dot 5** Begins initial-letter contraction.
• • • • • ●	**dot 6** Capitalization sign; the whole word is capitalized when this sign is doubled.

1 CELL, 2 DOTS

● • ● • • •	**1-2** **b** **but** Single-letter contraction. May be used as a whole-word contraction only; may be followed by an apostrophe. **2** (when preceded by the number sign).

1-3
k
knowledge Single-letter contraction. May be used as a whole-word contraction only.

1-4
c
can Single-letter contraction. May be used as a whole-word contraction only; may be followed by an apostrophe.
3 (when preceded by the number sign).

1-5
e
every Single-letter contraction. May be used as a whole-word contraction only.
5 (when preceded by the number sign).

1-6
ch Part-word contraction.
child Whole-word contraction only. May be followed by an apostrophe.

2-3
be Part- or whole-word contraction.
bb Part-word contraction.
; Semicolon.

2-4
i
9 (when preceded by the number sign).

2-5
con Part-word contraction.
cc Part-word contraction.
: Colon.

2-6
en Part-word contraction.
enough Whole-word contraction only.

3-4
st Part-word contraction or abbreviation.
still Whole-word contraction only. May be followed by an apostrophe.
/ Slash.

3-5
in Part- or whole-word contraction.

3-6
com Part-word contraction.
- Hyphen; dash when sign is doubled.

4-5
Begins a part- or a whole-word contraction.

4-6
Begins a part-word contraction.
Italic, underline, or bold sign.
. Decimal point.

5-6
Letter sign.
Begins a part-word contraction.

1 CELL, 3 DOTS

1-2-3
l
like Single-letter contraction. May be used as a whole-word contraction only.

1-2-4
f
from Single-letter contraction. May be used as a whole-word contracton only.
6 (when preceded by the number sign).

1-2-5
h
have Single-letter contraction. May be used as a whole-word contraction only.
8 (when preceded by the number sign).

1-2-6
gh Part-word contraction only.

1-3-4
m
more Single-letter contraction. May be used as a whole-word contraction only.

1-3-5
o

1-3-6
u
us Single-letter contraction. May be used as a whole-word contraction only.

1-4-5
d
do Single-letter contraction. May be used as a whole-word contraction only.
4 (when preceded by the number sign).

1-4-6
sh Part-word contraction.
shall Whole-word contraction only.

1-5-6
wh Part-word contraction.
which Whole-word contraction only.

2-3-4
s
so Whole-word contraction only. May be followed by an apostrophe.

2-3-5
to Whole-word contraction only. There will be no space between this symbol and the word, composition sign, or symbol that follows.
ff Part-word contraction. Will be found in the middle of the word only.
! Exclamation mark.

2-3-6
his Whole-word contraction only.
? Question mark.
" Opening quotation mark.
' Opening single quotation mark when preceded by dot 6.

2-4-5
j
just Whole-word contraction only.
0 (when preceded by the number sign).

2-4-6
ow Part-word contraction.

2-5-6
dis Part-word contraction.
dd Part-word contraction.
. Period.
$ Dollar sign.

3-4-5
ar Part-word contraction.

3-4-6
ing Part-word contraction.

3-5-6
by Whole-word contraction only. There will be no space between this symbol and the word, composition sign, or symbol that follows.
was Whole-word contraction only.
" Closing quotation mark.
' Closing single quotation mark when followed by dot 3.

4-5-6
Begins a part- or a whole-word contraction.

1 CELL, 4 DOTS

1-2-3-4
p
people Whole-word contraction only. May be followed by an apostrophe.

1-2-3-5
r
rather Whole-word contraction only.

1-2-3-6
v
very Whole-word contraction only.

1-2-4-5
g
go Whole-word contraction only.
7 (when preceded by the number sign).

1-2-4-6
ed Part-word contraction.

1-2-5-6
ou Part-word contraction.
out Whole-word contraction only.

1-3-4-5
n
not Whole-word contraction only.

1-3-4-6
x
it Whole-word contraction only. May be followed by an apostrophe.

1-3-5-6
z
as Whole-word contraction only.

1-4-5-6
th Part-word contraction.
this Whole-word contraction only.

2-3-4-5
t
that Whole-word contraction only. May be followed by an apostrophe.

2-3-4-6
the Part- or whole-word contraction.

2-3-5-6
were Whole-word contraction only.
gg Part-word contraction.
(Opening parenthesis.
) Closing parenthesis.
[Opening bracket (when preceded by dot 6).
] Closing bracket (when followed by dot 3).

2-4-5-6
w
will Whole-word contraction only.

3-4-5-6
ble Part-word contraction.
Number sign.

1 CELL, 5 DOTS

1-2-3-4-5
q
quite Whole-word contraction only.

1-2-3-4-6
and Part- or whole-word contraction.

1-2-3-5-6
of Part- or whole-word contraction.

1-2-4-5-6
er Part-word contraction only.

1-3-4-5-6
y
you Whole-word contraction only; may be followed by an apostrophe.

2-3-4-5-6
with Part- or whole-word contraction.

1 CELL, 6 DOTS

1-2-3-4-5-6
for Part- or whole-word contraction.

2 CELLS, 1 DOT

1, 1-2
about Short-form word. May be used as a part- or whole-word contraction.

1, 1-4
according Short-form word. May be used as a part- or whole-word contraction.

1, 1-2-3
also Short-form word. May be used as a part- or whole-word contraction.

1, 1-2-4
after Short-form word. May be used as a part- or whole-word contraction.

1, 1-2-4-5
again Short-form word. May be used as a part- or whole-word contraction.

5, 1-3
know Part- or whole-word contraction.

5, 1-5
ever Part- or whole-word contraction.

5, 1-6
character Part- or whole-word contraction.

5, 1-2-3
lord Part- or whole-word contraction.

5, 1-2-4
father Part- or whole-word contraction.

5, 1-2-5
here Part- or whole-word contraction.

5, 1-3-4
mother Part- or whole-word contraction.

5, 1-3-5
one Part- or whole-word contraction.

5, 1-3-6
under Part- or whole-word contraction.

5, 1-4-5
day Part- or whole-word contraction.

5, 1-5-6
where Part- or whole-word contraction.

5, 2-3-4
some Part- or whole-word contraction.

5, 1-2-3-4
part Part- or whole-word contraction.

5, 1-2-3-5
right Part- or whole-word contraction.

5, 1-2-5-6
ought Part- or whole-word contraction.

5, 1-3-4-5
name Part- or whole word contraction.

5, 1-4-5-6
through Part- or whole-word contraction.

5, 2-3-4-5
time Part- or whole-word contraction.

5, 2-3-4-6
there Part- or whole-word contraction.

5, 2-4-5-6
work Part- or whole-word contraction.

5, 1-2-3-4-5
question Part- or whole-word contraction.

5, 1-3-4-5-6
young Part- or whole-word contraction.

6, 3
Termination sign.
Transcriber's note (begin and end).

6, 1-3-4-5
ation Part-word contraction.

6, 1-3-4-5-6
ally Part-word contraction.

6, 2-3-5-6
[Bracket-brace (opening).

2 CELLS, 2 DOTS

1-2, 1-2-3
blind Short-form word. May be used as a part- or whole-word contraction.

1-4, 1-4-5
could Short-form word. May be used as a part- or whole-word contraction.

1-5, 2-4
either Short-form word. May be used as a part- or whole-word contraction.

1-6, 1-3-4-5
children Short-form word. May be used as a part- or whole-word contraction.

2-3, 1-4
because Short-form word. May be used as a part- or whole-word contraction.

2-3, 1-2-3
below Short-form word. May be used as a part- or whole-word contraction.

2-3, 1-2-4
before Short-form word. May be used as a part- or whole-word contraction.

2-3, 1-2-5
behind Short-form word. May be used as a part- or whole-word contraction.

2-3, 2-3-4
beside Short-form word. May be used as a part- or whole-word contraction.

2-3, 1-3-4-5
beneath Short-form word. May be used as a part- or whole-word contraction.

2-3, 2-3-4-5
between Short-form word. May be used as a part- or whole-word contraction.

2-3, 1-3-4-5-6
beyond Short-form word. May be used as a part- or whole-word contraction.

2-5, 1-2-3-4
% Percent.

3-5, 3-5
* Asterisk.

3-5, 2-3-5
into Whole-word contraction only. There will be no space between this symbol and the word, composition sign, or symbol that follows.

3-6, 3-6
— Dash.

4-5, 1-3-6
upon Part- or whole-word contraction.

4-5, 1-5-6
whose Part- or whole-word contraction.

4-5, 1-4-5-6
those Part- or whole-word contraction.

4-5, 2-3-4-6
these Part- or whole-word contraction.

4-5, 2-4-5-6
word Part- or whole-word contraction.

4-6, 1-5
ance Part-word contraction.

4-6, 1-4-5
ound Part-word contraction.

4-6, 2-3-4
less Part-word contraction.

4-6, 1-3-4-5
sion Part-word contraction.

4-6, 2-3-4-5
ount Part-word contraction.

5-6, 1-5
ence Part-word contraction.

5-6, 1-2-3
ful Part-word contraction.

5-6, 2-3-4
ness Part-word contraction.

5-6, 1-2-4-5
ong Part-word contraction.

5-6, 1-3-4-5
tion Part-word contraction.

5-6, 1-3-4-5-6
ity Part-word contraction.

5-6, 2-3-4-5
ment Part-word contraction.

2 CELLS, 3 DOTS

1-2-3, 1-2-3
little Short-form word. May be used as a part- or whole-word contraction.

1-2-3, 1-2-3-5
letter Short-form word. May be used as a part- or whole-word contraction.

1-2-4, 1-2-3-5
friend Short-form word. May be used as a part- or whole-word contraction.

1-2-4, 3-4
first Short-form word. May be used as a part- or whole-word contraction.

1-2-5, 1-3-4
him Short-form word. May be used as a part- or whole-word contraction.

1-3-4, 1-6
much Short-form word. May be used as a part- or whole-word contraction.

1-3-4, 3-4
must Short-form word. May be used as a part- or whole-word contraction.

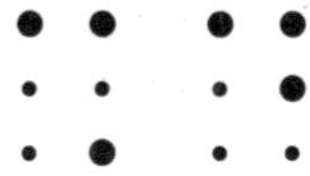

1-4-6, 1-4-5
should Short-form word. May be used as a part- or whole-word contraction.

2-3-4, 1-6
such Short-form word. May be used as a part- or whole-word contraction.

2-3-4, 1-4-5
said Short-form word. May be used as a part- or whole-word contraction.

4-5-6, 1-4
cannot Part- or whole word contraction.

4-5-6, 1-2-5
had Part- or whole-word contraction.

4-5-6, 1-3-4
many Part- or whole-word contraction.

4-5-6, 2-3-4
spirit Part- or whole-word contraction.

4-5-6, 2-3-4-6
their Part- or whole-word contraction.

4-5-6, 2-4-5-6
world Part- or whole-word contraction.

2 CELLS, 4 DOTS

1-2-3-4, 1-4-5
paid Short-form word. May be used as a part- or whole-word contraction.

1-2-4-5, 1-4-5
good Short-form word. May be used as a part- or whole-word contraction.

1-3-4-6, 2-3-4
its Short-form word. May be used as a part- or whole-word contraction.

1-3-4-6, 1-2-4
itself Short-form word. May be used as a part- or whole-word contraction.

2-3-4-5, 1-3-4
tomorrow Short-form word. May be used as a part- or whole-word contraction.

2-3-4-5, 1-4-5
today Short-form word. May be used as a part- or whole-word contraction.

2-3-4-5, 1-3-4-5
tonight Short-form word. May be used as a part- or whole-word contraction.

2-3-5-6, 3
] Bracket-brace (closing).

2-4-5-6, 1-4-5
would Short-form word. May be used as a part- or whole-word contraction.

2 CELLS, 5 DOTS

1-2-3-4-5, 1-3
quick Short-form word. May be used as a part- or whole-word contraction.

1-3-4-5-6, 1-2-3-5
your Short-form word. May be used as a part- or whole-word contraction.

3 CELLS, 1 DOT

1, 1-2, 1-2-3-6
above Short-form word. May be used as a part- or whole-word contraction.

1, 1-4, 1-2-3-5
across Short-form word. May be used as a part- or whole-word contraction.

1, 1-2-3, 1-3-4
almost Short-form word. May be used as a part- or whole-word contraction.

1, 1-2-3, 1-2-3-5
already Short-form word. May be used as a part- or whole-word contraction.

1, 1-2-3, 1-4-5-6
although Short-form word. May be used as a part- or whole-word contraction.

1, 1-2-3, 2-3-4-5
altogether Short-form word. May be used as a part- or whole-word contraction.

1, 1-2-3, 2-4-5-6
always Short-form word. May be used as a part- or whole-word contraction.

1, 1-2-4, 1-3-4-5
afternoon Short-form word. May be used as a part- or whole-word contraction.

1, 1-2-4, 2-4-5-6
afterward Short-form word. May be used as a part- or whole-word contraction.

1, 1-2-4-5, 3-4
against Short-form word. May be used as a part- or whole-word contraction.

3, 3, 3
. . . Ellipsis.

5, 1-3-5, 1-2-4
oneself Short-form word. May be used as a part- or whole-word contraction.

3 CELLS, 2 DOTS

1-2, 1-2-3-5, 1-2-3
braille Short-form word. May be used as a part- or whole-word contraction.

2-4, 1-3-4, 1-3-4
immediate Short-form word. May be used as a part- or whole-word contraction.

2-5, 1-4, 1-2-3-6
conceive Short-form word. May be used as a part- or whole-word contraction.

3 CELLS, 3 DOTS

1-2-5, 1-3-4, 1-2-4
himself Short-form word. May be used as a part- or whole-word contraction.

1-2-5, 1-2-4-5-6, 1-2-4
herself Short-form word. May be used as a part- or whole-word contraction.

1-3-4, 1-3-4-5-6, 1-2-4
myself Short-form word. May be used as a part- or whole-word contraction.

1-3-5, 3, 1-4
o'clock Short-form word. May be used as a part- or whole-word contraction.

1-4-5, 1-4, 1-2-3
declare Short-form word. May be used as a part- or whole-word contraction.

1-4-5, 1-4, 1-2-3-6
deceive Short-form word. May be used as a part- or whole-word contraction.

3 CELLS, 4 DOTS

1-2-3-4, 1-2-4-5-6, 1-2-5
perhaps Short-form word. May be used as a part- or whole-word contraction.

1-2-3-5, 1-4, 1-2-3-6
receive Short-form word. May be used as a part- or whole-word contraction.

1-2-3-5, 2-4-5, 1-4
rejoice Short-form word. May be used as a part- or whole-word contraction.

1-2-4-5, 1-2-3-5, 2-3-4-5
great Short-form word. May be used as a part- or whole-word contraction.

1-3-4-5, 1-5, 1-4
necessary Short-form word. May be used as a part- or whole-word contraction.

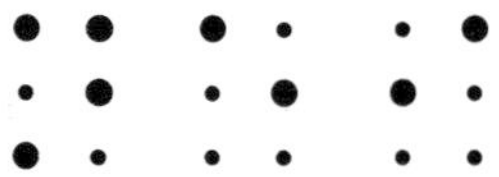

1-3-4-5, 1-5, 2-4
neither Short-form word. May be used as a part- or whole-word contraction.

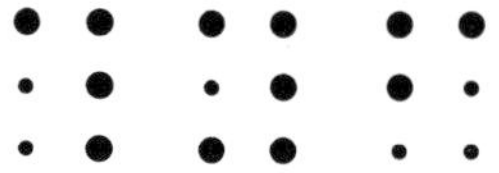

1-4-5-6, 1-3-4-5-6, 1-2-4
thyself Short-form word. May be used as a part- or whole-word contraction.

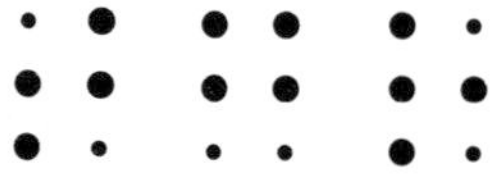

2-3-4-5, 1-2-4-5, 1-2-3-5
together Short-form word. May be used as a part- or whole-word contraction.

3 CELLS, 5 DOTS

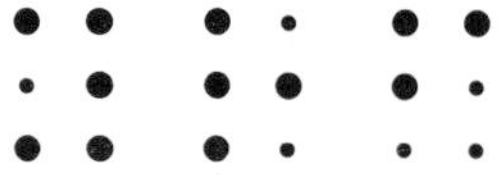

1-3-4-5-6, 1-2-3-5, 1-2-4
yourself Short-form word. May be used as a part- or whole-word contraction.

4 CELLS, 2 DOTS

2-5, 1-4, 1-2-3-6, 1-2-4-5
conceiving Short-form word. May be used as a part- or whole-word contraction.

4 CELLS, 3 DOTS

1-4-5, 1-4, 1-2-3, 1-2-4-5
declaring Short-form word. May be used as a part- or whole-word contraction.

1-4-5, 1-4, 1-2-3-6, 1-2-4-5
deceiving Short-form word. May be used as a part- or whole-word contraction.

4 CELLS, 4 DOTS

1-2-3-4, 1-2-4-5-6, 1-4, 1-2-3-6
perceive Short-form word. May be used as a part- or whole-word contraction.

1-2-3-5, 1-4, 1-2-3-6, 1-2-4-5
receiving Short-form word. May be used as a part- or whole-word contraction.

1-2-3-5, 2-4-5, 1-4, 1-2-4-5
rejoicing Short-form word. May be used as a part- or whole-word contraction.

1-2-5-6, 1-2-3-5, 1-2-3-6, 2-3-4
ourselves Short-form word. May be used as a part- or whole-word contraction.

2-3-4-6, 1-3-4, 1-2-3-6, 2-3-4
themselves Short-form word. May be used as a part- or whole-word contraction.

4 CELLS, 5 DOTS

1-3-4-5-6, 1-2-3-5, 1-2-3-6, 2-3-4
yourselves Short-form word. May be used as a part- or whole-word contraction.

5 CELLS, 4 DOTS

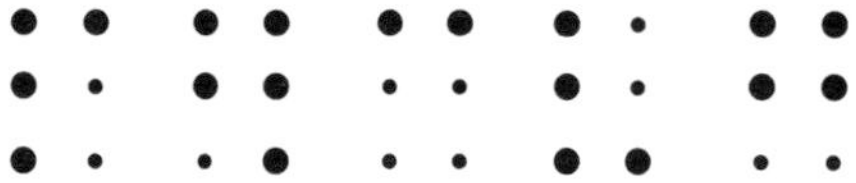

1-2-3-4, 1-2-4-5-6, 1-4, 1-2-3-6, 1-2-4-5
perceiving Short-form word. May be used as a part- or whole-word contraction.

Print to Braille

This section alphabetically lists all contractions and symbols used in braille and briefly describes the rules that pertain to them. Not all the rules are included here; only those that are commonly used have been included.

a—dot 1

Must be preceded by a letter sign when representing a single letter (not including the word *a*).

about—ab

Short-form word, part- or whole-word contraction. May be used to represent an entire proper name, but not as a part-word contraction in a proper name. May not be divided between lines.

above—abv

Short-form word, part- or whole-word contraction. May be used to represent an entire proper name, but not as a part-word contraction in a proper name. May not be divided between lines.

according—ac

Short-form word, part- or whole-word contraction. May be used to represent an entire proper name, but not as a part-word contraction in a proper name. May not be divided between lines.

across—acr

Short-form word, part- or whole-word contraction. May be used to represent an entire proper name, but not as a part-word contraction in a proper name. May not be divided between lines.

after—af

Short-form word, part- or whole-word contraction. May be used to represent an entire proper name, but not as a part-word contraction in a proper name. Cannot be followed by a vowel when used as a part-word contraction. May not be divided between lines.

afternoon—afn

Short-form word, part- or whole-word contraction. May be used to represent an entire proper name, but not as a part-word contraction in a proper name. May not be divided between lines.

afterward—afw

Short-form word, part- or whole-word contraction. May be used to represent an entire proper name, but not as a part-word contraction in a proper name. May not be divided between lines.

again—ag
Short-form word, part- or whole-word contraction. May be used to represent an entire proper name, but not as a part-word contraction in a proper name. May not be divided between lines.

against—ag(st)
Short-form word, part- or whole-word contraction. May be used to represent an entire proper name, but not as a part-word contraction in a proper name. May not be divided between lines.

ally—dots 6, 1-3-4-5-6
Final-letter contraction, part-word contraction only. Can be used only in the middle or at the end of a word. Cannot begin a word or directly follow a prefix, an apostrophe, or a hyphen. Can begin a new line in a divided word.

almost—alm
Short-form word, part- or whole-word contraction. May be used to represent an entire proper name, but not as a part-word contraction in a proper name. May not be divided between lines.

already—alr
Short-form word, part- or whole-word contraction. May be used to represent an entire proper name, but not as a part-word contraction in a proper name. May not be divided between lines.

also—al
Short-form word, part- or whole-word contraction. May be used to represent an entire proper name, but not as a part-word contraction in a proper name. May not be divided between lines.

although—al(th)
Short-form word, part- or whole-word contraction. May be used to represent an entire proper name, but not as a part-word contraction in a proper name. May not be divided between lines.

altogether—alt
Short-form word, part- or whole-word contraction. May be used to represent an entire proper name, but not as a part-word contraction in a proper name. May not be divided between lines.

always—alw

Short-form word, part- or whole-word contraction. May be used to represent an entire proper name, but not as a part-word contraction in a proper name. May not be divided between lines.

ance—dots 4-6, 1-5

Final-letter contraction, part-word contraction only. Can be used only in the middle or at the end of a word. Cannot begin a word or directly follow a prefix, an apostrophe, or a hyphen. Can begin a new line in a divided word.

and—dots 1-2-3-4-6

Whole-word contraction. When used as a whole-word contraction, there should be no space between *and* and the words *a, for, of, the,* and *with* unless separated by punctuation or composition signs.

Part-word contraction. Can be used as a part-word contraction wherever the letters occur. Cannot be used when separated by a prefix and a root.

ar—dots 3-4-5

Part-word contraction. Cannot be used when separated by components of compound words.

as—z

Whole-word contraction only.

ation—dots 6, 1-3-4-5

Final-letter contraction, part-word contraction only. Can be used only in the middle or at the end of a word. Cannot begin a word or directly follow a prefix, an apostrophe, or a hyphen. Can begin a new line in a divided word.

b—dots 1-2

Must be preceded by a letter sign when representing a single letter.

bb—dots 2-3

Double-letter contraction, part-word contraction. Can be used only between letters or contraction within a word. Cannot be used in contact with punctuation, including a hyphen and an apostrophe, or when separated by components of compound words. All other one-cell contractions have precedence.

be—dots 2-3

Whole-word lower-sign contraction. Cannot be used in contact with another letter, contraction, word, or punctuation sign, except the capital-letter and italic, bold, and underline signs.

Part-word lower-sign contraction. Can be used only when it constitutes a syllable at the beginning of a word or line. Can be preceded by a hyphen, but cannot be followed by one or by an apostrophe.

because—(be)c

Short-form word, part- or whole-word contraction. May be used to represent an entire proper name, but not as a part-word contraction in a proper name. May not be divided between lines.

before—(be)f

Short-form word, part- or whole-word contraction. May be used to represent an entire proper name, but not as a part-word contraction in a proper name. May not be divided between lines.

behind—(be)h

Short-form word, part- or whole-word contraction. May be used to represent an entire proper name, but not as a part-word contraction in a proper name. May not be divided between lines.

below—(be)l

Short-form word, part- or whole-word contraction. May be used to represent an entire proper name, but not as a part-word contraction in a proper name. May not be divided between lines.

beneath—(be)n

Short-form word, part- or whole-word contraction. May be used to represent an entire proper name, but not as a part-word contraction in a proper name. May not be divided between lines.

beside—(be)s

Short-form word, part- or whole-word contraction. May be used to represent an entire proper name, but not as a part-word contraction in a proper name. May not be divided between lines.

between—(be)t

Short-form word, part- or whole-word contraction. May be used to represent an entire proper name, but not as a part-word contraction in a proper name. May not be divided between lines.

beyond—(be)y

Short-form word, part- or whole-word contraction. May be used to represent an entire proper name, but not as a part-word contraction in a proper name. May not be divided between lines.

ble—dots 3-4-5-6

Part-word contraction. Cannot be used when separated by components of compound words or at the beginning of a word.

blind—bl

Short-form word, part- or whole-word contraction. May be used to represent an entire proper name, but not as a part-word contraction in a proper name. Cannot be followed by a vowel when used as a part-word contraction.

braille—brl

Short-form word, part- or whole-word contraction. May be used to represent an entire proper name, but not as a part-word contraction in a proper name.

but—b

Single-letter contraction, whole-word contraction only. Can be used in contact with punctuation, including a hyphen.

by—dots 3-5-6

Whole-word lower-sign contraction, whole-word contraction only. No space should be left between *by* and the word, composition sign, or symbol (dollar sign, percent sign, and so forth) following it. Can be preceded or followed by a capital-letter or an italic, bold, or underline sign. Cannot be followed by punctuation.

c—dots 1-4

Must be preceded by a letter sign when representing a single letter.

can—c

Single-letter contraction, whole-word contraction only. Can be used in contact with punctuation, including a hyphen. Can be followed by an apostrophe in the words *can's* and *can't* only.

cannot—dots 4-5-6, 1-4

Initial-letter contraction. Can be used as a part- or a whole-word contraction when it retains its original sound.

cc—dots 2-5

Double-letter contraction, part-word contraction. Can be used only between letters or contraction within a word. Cannot be used in contact with punctuation, including a hyphen and an apostrophe, or when separated by components of compound words; all other one-cell contractions have precedence.

ch—dots 1-6

Part-word contraction. Can be used in contact with punctuation, including a hyphen and an apostrophe. Cannot be used when separated by a prefix and a root or between components of compound words.

character—dots 5, 1-6

Initial-letter contraction. Can be used as a part- or a whole-word contraction when it retains its original sound.

child—(ch)

Whole-word contraction only. Can be used in contact with punctuation and composition signs. Cannot be used with an apostrophe (except with the word *child's*).

children—(ch)n

Short-form word, part- or whole-word contraction. May be used to represent an entire proper name, but not as a part-word contraction in a proper name. May not be divided between lines.

com—dots 3-6

Part-word lower-sign contraction. Can be used only at the beginning of a word or line. Can never be used in contact with a hyphen, a dash, or an apostrophe.

con—dots 2-5

Part-word lower-sign contraction. Can be used only when it constitutes a syllable at the beginning of a word or line. Can be preceded by a hyphen, but not followed by one. Cannot be followed by an apostrophe.

conceive—(con)cv

Short-form word, part- or whole-word contraction. May be used to represent an entire proper name, but not as a part-word contraction in a proper name. May not be divided between lines.

conceiving—(con)cvg

Short-form word, part- or whole-word contraction. May be used to represent an entire proper name, but not as a part-word contraction in a proper name. May not be divided between lines.

could—cd

Short-form word, part- or whole-word contraction. May be used to represent an entire proper name, but not as a part-word contraction in a proper name.

d—dots 1-4-5

Must be preceded by a letter sign when representing a single letter.

day—dots 5, 1-4-5

Initial-letter contraction. Can be used as a part- or a whole-word contraction when it retains its original sound.

dd—dots 2-5-6

Double-letter contraction, part-word contraction. Can be used only between letters or contractions within a word. Cannot be used in contact with punctuation, including a hyphen and an apostrophe, or when separated by components of a compound word; all other one-cell contractions have precedence.

deceive—dcv

Short-form word, part- or whole-word contraction. May be used to represent an entire proper name, but not as a part-word contraction in a proper name. May not be divided between lines.

deceiving—dcvg

Short-form word, part- or whole-word contraction. May be used to represent an entire proper name, but not as a part-word contraction in a proper name. May not be divided between lines.

declare—dcl

Short-form word, part- or whole-word contraction. May be used to represent an entire proper name, but not as a part-word contraction in a proper name. May not be divided between lines.

declaring—dclg

Short-form word, part- or whole-word contraction. May be used to represent an entire proper name, but not as a part-word contraction in a proper name. May not be divided between lines.

dis—dots 2-5-6

Part-word lower-sign contraction. Can be used only when it constitutes a syllable at the beginning of a word or line. Can be preceded by a hyphen, but not followed by one. Cannot be followed by an apostrophe.

do—d

Single-letter contraction, whole-word contraction only. Can be used in contact with punctuation, including a hyphen. Cannot be used in contact with an apostrophe.

e—dots 1-5

Must be preceded by a letter sign when representing a single letter.

ea—dot 2

Part-word contraction. Can be used only between letters or contractions within a word. Cannot be used in contact with punctuation, including a hyphen and an apostrophe, or when separated by components of compound words; all other one-cell contractions have precedence.

ed—dots 1-2-4-6

Part- or whole-word contraction. Cannot be used when separated by a prefix and a root or by components of compound words. Can be used as a proper name.

either—ei

Short-form word, part- or whole-word contraction. May be used to represent an entire proper name, but not as a part-word contraction in a proper name.

en—dots 2-6

Part-word lower-sign contraction. Cannot be used when separated by a prefix and a root or by components of compound words.

ence—dots 5-6, 1-5

Final-letter contraction, part-word contraction only. Can be used only in the middle or at the end of a word. Cannot begin a word or directly follow a prefix, an apostrophe, or a hyphen. Can begin a new line in a divided word.

enough—dots 2-6

Whole-word lower-sign contraction. Cannot be used in contact with another letter, contraction, word, or punctuation sign, except the capital-letter and italic, bold, and underline signs.

er—dots 1-2-4-5-6

Part- or whole-word contraction. Cannot be used when separated by a prefix and a root or by components of compound words.

ever—dots 5, 1-5

Initial-letter contraction. Can be used as a part- or a whole-word contraction when it retains its original sound.

every—e

Single-letter contraction, whole-word contraction only. Can be used in contact with punctuation, including a hyphen. Cannot be used in contact with an apostrophe.

f—dots 1-2-4

Must be preceded by a letter sign when representing a single letter.

father—dots 5, 1-2-4

Initial-letter contraction. Can be used as a part- or a whole-word contraction when it retains its original sound.

ff—dots 2-3-5

Double-letter contraction, part-word contraction. Can be used only between letters or contractions within a word. Cannot be used in contact with punctuation, including a hyphen and an apostrophe, or when separated by components of compound words; all other one-cell contractions have precedence.

first—f(st)

Short-form word, part- or whole-word contraction. May be used to represent an entire proper name, but not as a part-word contraction in a proper name.

for—dots 1-2-3-4-5-6

Whole-word contraction. When used as a whole-word contraction, there should be no space between *for* and the words *a, and, of, the,* and *with* unless separated by punctuation or composition signs.

Part-word contraction. Can be used as a part-word contraction wherever the letters occur, except when separated by a prefix and a root.

friend—fr
Short-form word, part- or whole-word contraction. May be used to represent an entire proper name, but not as a part-word contraction in a proper name. Cannot be followed by a vowel when used as a part-word contraction.

from—f
Single-letter contraction, whole-word contraction only. Can be used in contact with punctuation, including a hyphen. Cannot be used in contact with an apostrophe.

ful—dots 5-6, 1-2-3
Final-letter contraction, part-word contraction only. Can be used only in the middle or at the end of a word. Cannot begin a word or directly follow a prefix, an apostrophe, or a hyphen. Can begin a new line in a divided word.

g—dots 1-2-4-5
Must be preceded by a letter sign when representing a single letter.

gg—dots 2-3-5-6
Double-letter contraction, part-word contraction. Can be used only between letters or contractions within a word. Cannot be used in contact with punctuation, including a hyphen and an apostrophe, or when separated by components of compound words; all other one-cell contractions have precedence.

gh—dots 1-2-6
Part-word contraction. Cannot be used when placed between components of compound words.

go—g
Single-letter contraction, whole-word contraction only. Can be used in contact with punctuation, including a hyphen and an apostrophe.

good—gd
Short-form word, part- or whole-word contraction. May be used to represent an entire proper name, but not as a part-word contraction in a proper name.

great—grt
Short-form word, part- or whole-word contraction. May be used to represent an entire proper name, but not as a part-word contraction in a proper name.

h—dots 1-2-5
Must be preceded by a letter sign when representing a single letter.

had—dots 4-5-6, 1-2-5
Initial-letter contraction. Can be used as a part- or a whole-word contraction when it retains its original sound.

have—h
Single-letter contraction, whole-word contraction only.
Can be used in contact with punctuation, including a hyphen.
Cannot be used in contact with an apostrophe.

here—dots 5, 1-2-5
Inital-letter contraction. Can be used as a part- or a whole-word contraction when it retains its original sound.

herself—h(er)f
Short-form word, part- or whole-word contraction. May be used to represent an entire proper name, but not as a part-word contraction in a proper name. May not be divided between lines.

him—hm
Short-form word, part- or whole-word contraction. May be used to represent an entire proper name, but not as a part-word contraction in a proper name.

himself—hmf
Short-form word, part- or whole-word contraction. May be used to represent an entire proper name, but not as a part-word contraction in a proper name. May not be divided between lines.

his—dots 2-3-6
Whole-word lower-sign contraction. Cannot be used in contact with another letter, contraction, word, or punctuation sign, except the capital-letter and italic, bold, and underline signs.

i—dots 2-4
Must be preceded by a letter sign when representing a single letter (not including the word *I*).

immediate—imm

Short-form word, part- or whole-word contraction. May be used to represent an entire proper name, but not as a part-word contraction in a proper name.

in—dots 3-5

Whole-word lower-sign contraction. Cannot be used in contact with another letter, contraction, word, or punctuation sign, including a hyphen, except the capital-letter and italic, bold, and underline signs.

Part-word lower-sign contraction. Cannot be used when separated by a prefix and a root, by syllable breaks, or by components of compound words.

ing—dots 3-4-6

Part-word contraction. Cannot be used when separated by components of compound words or at the beginning of a word.

into—dots 3-5, 2-3-5

Whole-word lower-sign contraction, whole-word contraction only. No space should be left between *into* and the word, composition sign, or symbol (dollar sign, percent sign, and so on) following it. May be preceded or followed by a capital-letter or italic sign. Cannot be followed by punctuation.

it—x

Single-letter contraction, whole-word contraction only. Can be used in contact with punctuation, including a hyphen. Can be followed by an apostrophe in the words *it'd, it'll,* and *it's* only.

its—xs

Short-form word, part- or whole-word contraction. May be used to represent an entire proper name, but not as a part-word contraction in a proper name.

itself—xf

Short-form word, part- or whole-word contraction. May be used to represent an entire proper name, but not as a part-word contraction in a proper name. May not be divided between lines.

ity—dots 5-6, 1-3-4-5-6

Final-letter contraction, part-word contraction only. Can be used only in the middle or at the end of a word. Cannot begin a word or directly follow a prefix, an apostrophe, or a hyphen. Can begin a new line in a divided word.

j—dots 2-4-5

Must be preceded by a letter sign when representing a single letter.

just—j

Single-letter contraction, whole-word contraction only. Can be used in contact with punctuation, including a hyphen. Cannot be used in contact with an apostrophe.

k—dots 1-3

Must be preceded by a letter sign when representing a single letter.

know—dots 5, 1-3

Initial-letter contraction. Can be used as a part- or a whole-word contraction when it retains its original sound.

knowledge—k

Single-letter contraction, whole-word contraction only. Can be used in contact with punctuation, including a hyphen. Cannot be used in contact with an apostrophe.

l—dots 1-2-3

Must be preceded by a letter sign when representing a single letter.

less—dots 4-6, 2-3-4

Final-letter contraction, part-word contraction only. Can be used in the middle or at the end of a word. Cannot begin a word or directly follow a prefix, an apostrophe, or a hyphen. Can begin a new line in a divided word.

letter—lr

Short-form word, part- or whole-word contraction. May be used to represent an entire proper name, but not as a part-word contraction in a proper name.

like—l

Single-letter contraction, whole-word contraction only. Can be used in contact with punctuation, including a hyphen. Cannot be used in contact with an apostrophe.

little—ll
Short-form word, part- or whole-word contraction. May be used to represent an entire proper name, but not as a part-word contraction in a proper name.

lord—dots 5, 1-2-3
Initial-letter contraction. Can be used as a part- or a whole-word contraction when it retains its original sound.

m—dots 1-3-4
Must be preceded by a letter sign when representing a single letter.

many—dots 4-5-6, 1-3-4
Initial-letter contraction. Can be used as part- or a whole-word contraction when it retains its original sound.

ment—dots 5-6, 2-3-4-5
Final-letter contraction, part-word contraction only. Can be used only in the middle or at the end of a word. Cannot begin a word or directly follow a prefix, an apostrophe, or a hyphen. Can begin a new line in a divided word.

more—m
Single-letter contraction, whole-word contraction only. Can be used in contact with punctuation, including a hyphen. Cannot be used in contact with an apostrophe.

mother—dots 5, 1-3-4
Initial-letter contraction. Can be used as a part- or a whole-word contraction when it retains its original sound.

much—m(ch)
Short-form word, part- or whole-word contraction. May be used to represent an entire proper name, but not as a part-word contraction in a proper name.

must—m(st)
Short-form word, part- or whole-word contraction. May be used tc represent an entire proper name, but not as a part-word contraction in a proper name.

myself—myf

Short-form word, part- or whole-word contraction. May be used to represent an entire proper name, but not as a part-word contraction in a proper name. May not be divided between lines.

n—dots 1-3-4-5

Must be preceded by a letter sign when representing a single letter.

name—dots 5, 1-3-4-5

Initial-letter contraction. Can be used as a part- or a whole-word contraction when it retains its original sound.

necessary—nec

Short-form word, part- or whole-word contraction. May be used to represent an entire proper name, but not as a part-word contraction in a proper name.

neither—nei

Short-form word, part- or whole-word contraction. May be used to represent an entire proper name, but not as a part-word contraction in a proper name.

ness—dots 5-6, 2-3-4

Final-letter contraction, part-word contraction only. Can be used only in the middle or at the end of a word. Cannot begin a word or directly follow a prefix, an apostrophe, or a hyphen. Can begin a new line in a divided word.

not—n

Single-letter contraction, whole-word contraction only. Can be used in contact with punctuation, including a hyphen. Cannot be used in contact with an apostrophe.

o—dots 1-3-5

Must be preceded by a letter sign when representing a single letter.

o'clock—o'c

Short-form word, part- or whole-word contraction. May be used to represent an entire proper name, but not as a part-word contraction in a proper name. May not be divided between lines.

of—dots 1-2-3-5-6

Whole-word contraction. When used as a whole-word contraction, there should be no space between *of* and the words *a, and, for, the,* and *with* unless separated by punctuation or composition signs.

Part-word contraction. Can be used as a part-word contraction where the letters occur, cannot be used when separated by a prefix and a root, by syllable breaks, or by components of compound words.

one—dots 5, 1-3-5

Initial-letter contraction. Can be used as a part- or a whole-word contraction whenever the *o* and *n* are in the same syllable.

oneself—(one)f

Short-form word, part- or whole-word contraction. May be used to represent an entire proper name, but not as a part-word contraction in a proper name. May not be divided between lines.

ong—dots 5-6, 1-2-4-5

Final-letter contraction, part-word contraction only. Can be used only in the middle or at the end of a word. Cannot begin a word or directly follow a prefix, an apostrophe, or a hyphen. Can begin a new line in a divided word.

ou—dots 1-2-5-6

Part-word contraction. Can be used in contact with punctuation, including a hyphen and an apostrophe. Cannot be used when separated by a prefix and a root or between components of compound words.

ought—dots 5, 1-2-5-6

Initial-letter contraction. Can be used as a part- or a whole-word contraction when it retains its original sound.

ound—dots 4-6, 1-4-5

Final-letter contraction, part-word contraction only. Can be used only in the middle or at the end of a word. Cannot begin a word or directly follow a prefix, an apostrophe, or a hyphen. Can begin a new line in a divided word.

ount—dots 4-6, 2-3-4-5

Final-letter contraction, part-word contraction only. Can be used only in the middle or at the end of a word. Cannot begin a word or directly follow a prefix, an apostrophe, or a hyphen. Can begin a new line in a divided word.

ourselves—(ou)rvs
Short-form word, part- or whole-word contraction. May be used to represent an entire proper name, but not as a part-word contraction in a proper name. May not be divided between lines.

out—(ou)
Whole-word contraction only. Can be used in contact with punctuation and composition signs, except the apostrophe.

ow—dots 2-4-6
Part-word contraction. Cannot be used when separated by components of compound words.

p—dots 1-2-3-4
Must be preceded by a letter sign when representing a single letter.

paid—pd
Short-form word, part- or whole-word contraction. May be used to represent an entire proper name, but not as a part-word contraction in a proper name.

part—dots 5, 1-2-3-4
Initial-letter contraction. Can be used as a part- or a whole-word contraction unless the prefix *par* is followed by any form of the word *take*.

people—p
Single-letter contraction, whole-word contraction only. Can be used in contact with punctuation, including a hyphen. Can be followed by an apostrophe in the word *people's* only.

perceive—p(er)cv
Short-form word, part- or whole-word contraction. May be used to represent an entire proper name, but not as a part-word contraction in a proper name. May not be divided between lines.

perceiving—p(er)cvg
Short-form word, part- or whole-word contraction. May be used to represent an entire proper name, but not as a part-word contraction in a proper name. May not be divided between lines.

perhaps—p(er)h
Short-form word, part- or whole-word contraction. May be used to represent an entire proper name, but not as a part-word contraction in a proper name. May not be divided between lines.

q—dots 1-2-3-4-5
Must be preceded by a letter sign when representing a single letter.

question—dots 5, 1-2-3-4-5
Initial-letter contraction. Can be used as a part- or a whole-word contraction when it retains its original sound.

quick—qk
Short-form word, part- or whole-word contraction. May be used to represent an entire proper name, but not as a part-word contraction in a proper name.

quite—q
Single-letter contraction, whole-word contraction only. Can be used in contact with punctuation, including a hyphen. Cannot be used in contact with an apostrophe.

r—dots 1-2-3-5
Must be preceded by a letter sign when representing a single letter.

rather—r
Single-letter contraction, whole-word contraction only. Can be used in contact with punctuation, including a hyphen. Cannot be used in contact with an apostrophe.

receive—rcv
Short-form word, part- or whole-word contraction. May be used to represent an entire proper name, but not as a part-word contraction in a proper name. May not be divided between lines.

receiving—rcvg
Short-form word, part- or whole-word contraction. May be used to represent an entire proper name, but not as a part-word contraction in a proper name. May not be divided between lines.

rejoice—rjc
Short-form word, part- or whole-word contraction. May be used to represent an entire proper name, but not as a part-word contraction in a proper name.

rejoicing—rjcg
Short-form word, part- or whole-word contraction. May be used to represent an entire proper name, but not as a part-word contraction in a proper name. May not be divided between lines.

right—dots 5, 1-2-3-5
Initial-letter contraction. Can be used as a part- or a whole-word contraction when it retains its original sound.

s—dots 2-3-4
Must be preceded by a letter sign when representing a single letter.

said—sd
Short-form word, part- or whole-word contraction. May be used to represent an entire proper name, but not as a part-word contraction in a proper name.

sh—dots 1-4-6
Part-word contraction. Can be used in contact with punctuation, including a hyphen and an apostrophe. Cannot be used when separated by a prefix and a root or between components of compound words.

shall—(sh)
Whole-word contraction only. Can be used in contact with punctuation and composition signs, except the apostrophe.

should—(sh)d
Short-form word, part- or whole-word contraction. May be used to represent an entire proper name, but not as a part-word contraction in a proper name.

sion—dots 4-6; 1-3-4-5
Final-letter contraction, part-word contraction only. Can be used only in the middle or at the end of a word. Cannot begin a word or directly follow a prefix, an apostrophe, or a hyphen. Can begin a new line in a divided word.

so—s
Single-letter contraction, whole-word contraction only. Can be used in contact with punctuation, including a hyphen. Can be followed by an apostrophe in the word *so's* only.

some—dots 5, 2-3-4
Initial-letter contraction. Can be used as a part- or a whole-word contraction when it retains its original sound and forms a complete syllable in the base word.

spirit—dots 4-5-6, 2-3-4

Initial-letter contraction. Can be used as a part- or a whole-word contraction when it retains its original sound.

st—dots 3-4

Part-word contraction. Can be used in contact with punctuation, including a hyphen and an apostrophe. Cannot be used when separated by a prefix and a root or between components of compound words. Can be used for abbreviations of words, such as *street* or *saint,* or in *1st*.

still—(st)

Whole-word contraction only. Can be used in contact with punctuation and composition signs. Cannot be used with an apostrophe (except with the word *still's* as in *John Still's book*).

such—s(ch)

Short-form word, part- or whole-word contraction. May be used to represent an entire proper names, but not as a part-word contraction in a proper name.

t—dots 2-3-4-5

Must be preceded by a letter sign when representing a single letter.

th—dots 1-4-5-6

Part-word contraction. Can be used in contact with punctuation, including a hyphen and an apostrophe. Cannot be used when separated by a prefix and a root or between components of compound words.

that—t

Single-letter contraction, whole-word contraction only. Can be used in contact with punctuation, including a hyphen. Can be followed by an apostrophe in the words *that'd, that'll,* and *that's* only.

the—dots 2-3-4-6

Whole-word contraction. When used as a whole-word contraction, there should be no space between *the* and the words *a, and, for, of,* and *with* unless separated by punctuation or composition signs.

Part-word contraction. Can be used as a part-word contraction wherever the letters occur. Cannot be used when separated by a prefix and a root, by syllable breaks, or by components of compound words.

their—dots 4-5-6, 2-3-4-6
Initial-letter contraction. Can be used as a part- or a whole-word contraction when it retains its original sound.

themselves—(the)mvs
Short-form word, part- or whole-word contraction. May be used to represent an entire proper name, but not as a part-word contraction in a proper name. May not be divided between lines.

there—dots 5, 2-3-4-6
Initial-letter contraction. Can be used as a part- or a whole-word contraction when it retains its original sound.

these—dots 4-5, 2-3-4-6
Initial-letter contraction. Can be used as a part- or a whole-word contraction when it retains its original sound.

this—(th)
Whole-word contraction only. Can be used in contact with punctuation and composition signs, except the apostrophe.

those—dots 4-5, 1-4-5-6
Initial-letter contraction. Can be used as a part- or a whole-word contraction when it retains its original sound.

through—dots 5, 1-4-5-6
Initial-letter contraction. Can be used as a part- or a whole-word contraction when it retains its original sound.

thyself—(th)yf
Short-form word, part- or whole-word contraction. May be used to represent an entire proper name, but not as a part-word contraction in a proper name. May not be divided between lines.

time—dots 5, 2-3-4-5
Initial letter contraction. Can be used as a part- or a whole-word contraction when it retains its original sound.

tion—dots 5-6, 1-3-4-5
Final letter contraction, part-word contraction only. Can be used only in the middle or at the end of a word. Cannot begin a

word nor directly follow a prefix, an apostrophe, or a hyphen. Can begin a new line in a divided word.

to—dots 2-3-5

Whole-word lower-sign contraction, whole-word contraction only. No space should be left between *to* and the word, composition sign, or symbol (dollar sign, percent sign, and so forth) following it. Can be preceded or followed by a capital-letter or an italic, bold, or underline sign. Cannot be followed by punctuation.

today/to-day—td

Short-form word, part- or whole-word contraction. May be used to represent an entire proper name, but not as a part-word contraction in a proper name.

together—tgr

Short-form word, part- or whole-word contraction. May be used to represent an entire proper name, but not as a part-word contraction in a proper name. May not be divided between lines.

tomorrow—tm

Short-form word, part- or whole-word contraction. May be used to represent an entire proper name, but not as a part-word contraction in a proper name.

tonight—tn

Short-form word, part- or whole-word contraction. May be used to represent an entire proper name, but not as a part-word contraction in a proper name.

u—dots 1-3-6

Must be preceded by a letter sign when representing a single letter.

under—dots 5, 1-3-6

Initial-letter contraction. Can be used as a part- or a whole-word contraction when it retains its original sound.

upon—dots 4-5, 1-3-6

Initial-letter contraction. Can be used as a part- or a whole-word contraction when it retains its original sound.

us—u

Single-letter contraction, whole-word contraction only. Can be used in contact with punctuation, including a hyphen. Cannot be used in contact with an apostrophe.

v—dots 1-2-3-6

Must be preceded by a letter sign when representing a single letter.

very—v

Single-letter contraction, whole-word contraction only. Can be used in contact with punctuation, including a hyphen. Cannot be used in contact with an apostrophe.

w—dots 2-4-5-6

Must be preceded by a letter sign when representing a single letter.

was—dots 3-5-6

Whole-word lower-sign contraction. Cannot be used in contact with another letter, contraction, word, or punctuation sign, except the capital-letter and italic, bold, and underline signs.

were—dots 2-3-5-6

Whole-word lower-sign contraction. Cannot be used in contact with another letter, contraction, word, or punctuation sign, except the capital-letter and italic, bold, and underline signs.

wh—dots 1-5-6

Part-word contraction. Can be used in contact with punctuation, including a hyphen and an apostrophe. Cannot be used when separated by a prefix and a root or between components of compound words.

where—dots 5, 1-5-6

Initial-letter contraction. Can be used as a part- or a whole-word contraction when it retains its original sound.

which—(wh)

Whole-word contraction only. Can be used in contact with punctuation and composition signs, except the apostrophe.

whose—dots 4-5, 1-5-6

Initial-letter contraction. Can be used as a part- or a whole-word contraction when it retains its original sound.

will—w

Single-letter contraction, whole-word contraction only. Can be used in contact with punctuation, including a hyphen. Can be followed by an apostrophe in the word *will's* only.

with—dots 2-3-4-5-6

Whole-word contraction. When used as a whole-word contraction, there should be no space between *with* and the words *a, and, for, of,* and *the* unless separated by punctuation or composition signs.

Part-word contraction. Can be used as a part-word contraction wherever the letters occur. Cannot be used when separated by a prefix and a root, by syllable breaks, or by components of compound words.

word—dots 4-5, 2-4-5-6

Initial-letter contraction. Can be used as a part- or a whole-word contraction when it retains its original sound.

work—dots 5, 2-4-5-6

Initial-letter contraction. Can be used as a part- or a whole-word contraction when it retains its original sound.

world—dots 4-5-6, 2-4-5-6

Initial-letter contraction. Can be used as a part- or a whole-word contraction when it retains its original sound.

would—wd

Short-form word, part- or whole-word contraction. May be used to represent an entire proper name, but not as a part-word contraction in a proper name.

x—dots 1-3-4-6

Must be preceded by a letter sign when representing a single letter.

y—dots 1-3-4-5-6

Must be preceded by a letter sign when representing a single letter.

you—y

Single-letter contraction, whole-word contraction only. Can be used in contact with punctuation, including a hyphen. Can be followed by an apostrophe in the words *you'd, you'll, you're,* and *you've.*

young—dots, 5, 1-3-4-5-6
Initial-letter contraction. Can be used as a part- or a whole-word contraction when it retains its original sound.

your—yr
Short-form word, part- or whole-word contraction. May be used to represent an entire proper name, but not as a part-word contraction in a proper name.

yourself—yrf
Short-form word, part- or whole-word contraction. May be used to represent an entire proper name, but not as a part-word contraction in a proper name. May not be divided between lines.

yourselves—yrvs
Short-form word, part- or whole-word contraction. May be used to represent an entire proper name, but not as a part-word contraction in a proper name. May not be divided between lines.

z—dots 1-3-5-6
Must be preceded by a letter sign when representing a single letter.

ABOUT THE AUTHOR

Mary F. Burns is an itinerant teacher of the visually impaired at Cooperative Educational Service Agency #6 (CESA #6) in Oshkosh, Wisconsin. She has been a brailler and certified teacher of braille since 1985.

The mission of the American Foundation for the Blind (AFB) is to enable persons who are blind or visually impaired to achieve equality of access and opportunity that will ensure freedom of choice in their lives. AFB accomplishes this mission by taking a national leadership role in the development and implementation of public policy and legislation, informational and educational programs, diversified products, and quality services. Among the services it provides, AFB maintains a national hotline to provide information and assistance to callers. The hotline number is 1-800-232-5463; it is in operation Mondays through Fridays, 8:30 a.m. to 4:30 p.m. EST or EDT.

It is the policy of the American Foundation for the Blind to use in the first printing of its books acid-free paper that meets the ANSI Z39.48 Standard. The infinity symbol that appears above indicates that the paper in this printing meets that standard.